His Name is Santorini

The story of a volcano

This book is dedicated to my beloved
husband who is always motivating
me towards new paths.

Note from the author

Santorini is our home and its unique character has inspired us in several ways. As a guide, I was trying once to explain the island`s geological history to some really young visitors and I came up with the story of Mr. Volcano. He was born about 2.5 million years ago and since then his numerous eruptions have been changing his shape and have added new layers of colorful rocks to his body.

The subduction of the tectonic plate of Africa under the Eurasian one, which is the reason for the volcanism in the Aegean sea, has been presented as a hug of Mama Africa and Papa Eurasio and the birth of a young volcano. His volcanic character and the different minerals that the lava contains are responsible for the dark colors of its rocks, grey, black, brown and red. The whitish upper layer is the volcanic dust that was deposited during the Minoan eruption.

The island`s long history and the human presence on it for about 6500 years appears as a successful marriage with his wife, Humanity.

During the illustration, Thomas was also inspired by the long history of the island and depicts Humanity with her characteristics in each era. The Crocus gatherer from the painting discovered in the prehistoric settlement of Akrotiri is an inspiration for Humanity when approaching Mr. Volcano for the first time. The swallows, the houses and boats of the time are also inspired by those depicted in paintings of the prehistoric Akrotiri. A few centuries after the Minoan eruption, the Spartans founded a colony on the island, so when Humanity comes back, she appears as a Spartan woman on an ancient Greek ship. And finally, she comes up as a modern hard working or relaxed woman nowadays.

The fertile soil of the volcano as well as the inventive ways that the inhabitants of it managed to use to cultivate several products, leaves no doubt that they are children of both Mr. Volcano and Humanity. As the vineyard of Santorini is one of the most ancient ones in Europe, the Assyrtiko grape appears as a very old sophisticated figure with white eyebrows, which produces one of the best white wines of the world!

We hope our story adds to a better understanding of the history of the island.

Enjoy it!
Dimitra Lola

His Name is Santorini

The story of a volcano

Once upon a time, millions of years ago, Mama Africa met Papa Eurasio. She submerged in his deep hug and their relationship gave birth to a little giant, baby Volcano.

Mama Africa adored her newborn
and kept on feeding him with
molten rock coming from the
deepest parts of her body.

Baby Volcano loved his home in the Aegean Sea and happy as he was and well fed, grew up fast.

He soon became a strong young
island-boy.

But like every adolescent, he could not always control his temper and he was often exploding, throwing out lava, tephra, and gases!

These were deposited on his surface adding a new layer every time. Thus he became a fully grown up Volcano, round and conical resembling a shield.

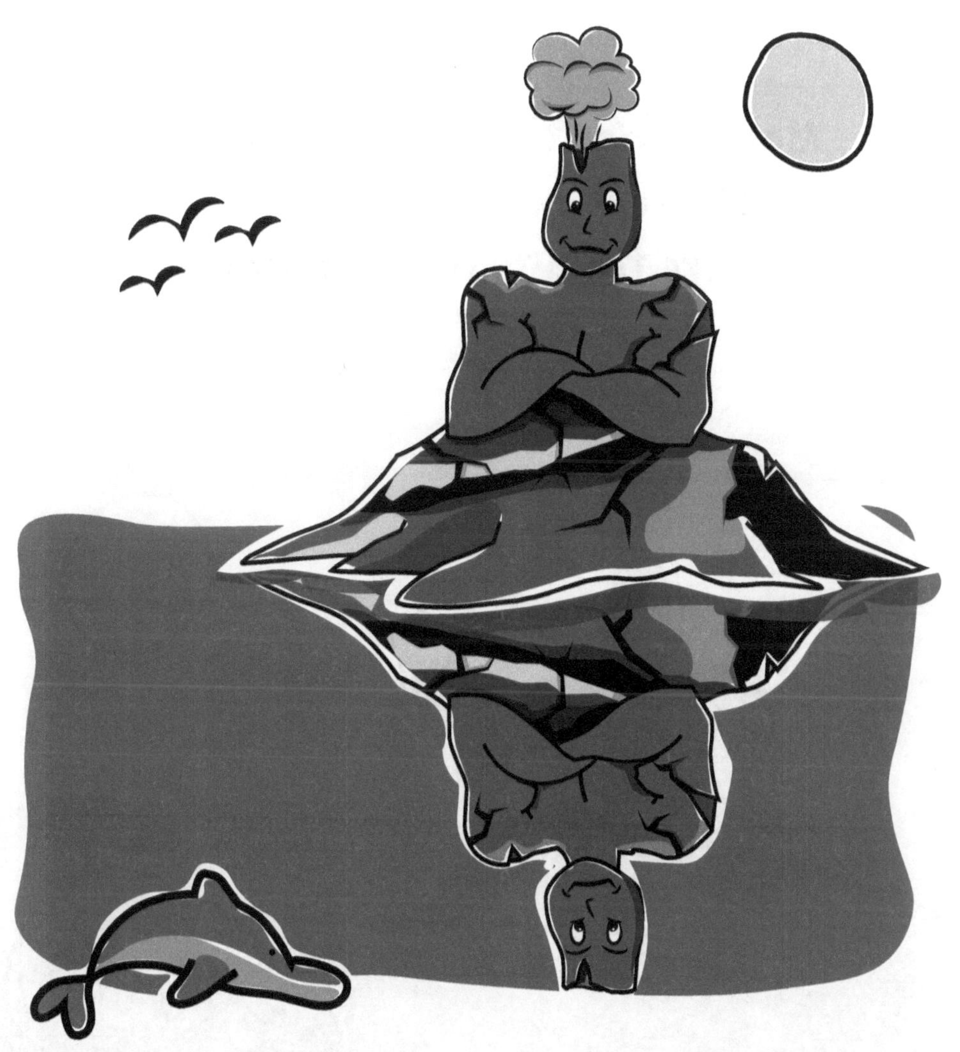

His wild beauty and various colors,
black, red, white, grey and a green
skin made him one of the most
impressive young islands on Earth.
He seemed awesome when mirrored in
the deep blue of the Aegean Sea!

Mama Africa though never let her son go. She kept on feeding him and there were times that he suffocated.

He then started exploding, hitting all
the islands around him and wiping
out not only everything on his way
but parts of himself as well.

These explosions often made him collapse and it took him some time to get back to the surface again. Simultaneously though he was becoming very creative, a true artist!

About 3600 years ago, during a period known as the Minoan, he was already married to Humanity, offering a fantastic environment for her to develop a very sophisticated civilization.

Their marriage was happy until
Mama Africa decided to interfere
again. That caused one of the worst
explosions of Mr. Volcano...

...so big that his wife, Humanity, left him and almost everything she had created with him was buried under his ashes.

That was one of the worst bursts
that Earth had faced. He was so
furious that he wasn't thinking that
he was losing almost half of his body
and his belly became like a cauldron
filled with sea water.

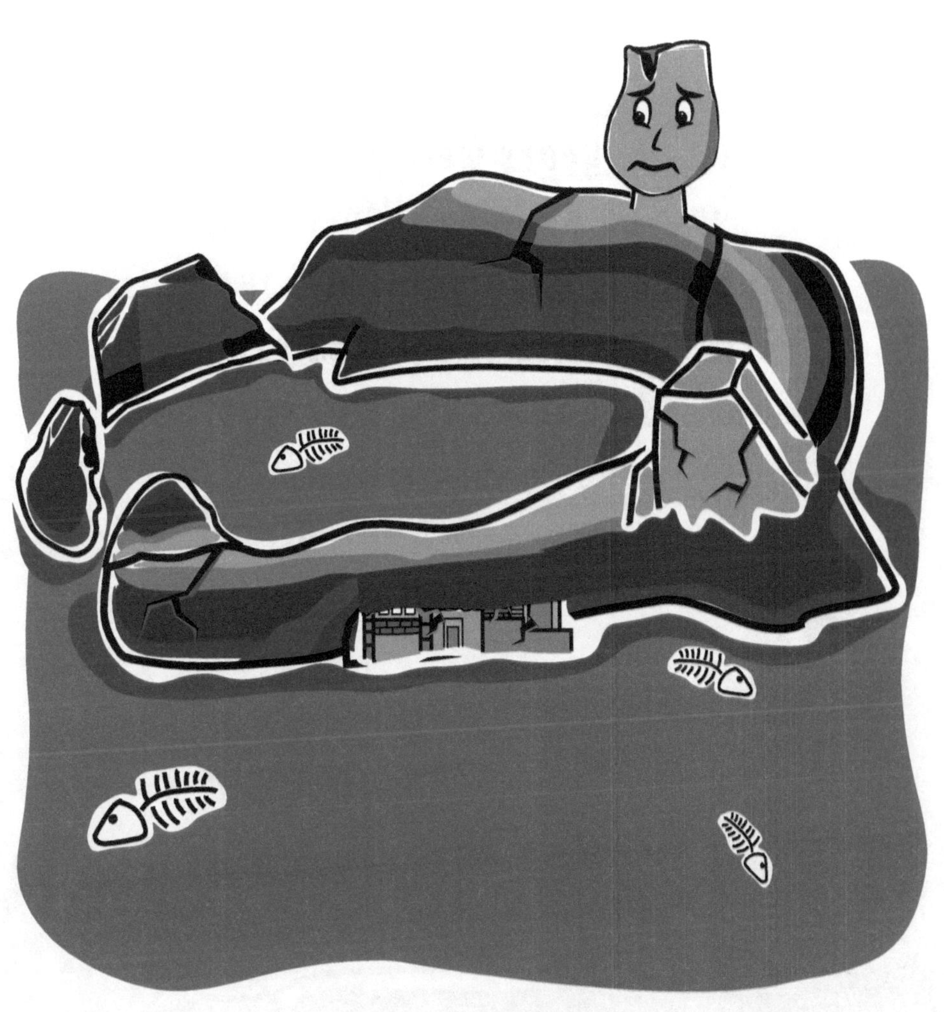

For many centuries everyone was
afraid of him and his body was toxic
to any sort of life.

But as the years were passing by, he calmed down and Humanity approached him again. Although his surface seemed rough and dry, she managed to tame him and together they gave birth to numerous children.

Each one of them got one of his colors.
Fava was the little one, cute, tasty and yellow.

Her sister, the Cherry Tomato, was the most beautiful, bright, juicy and red.

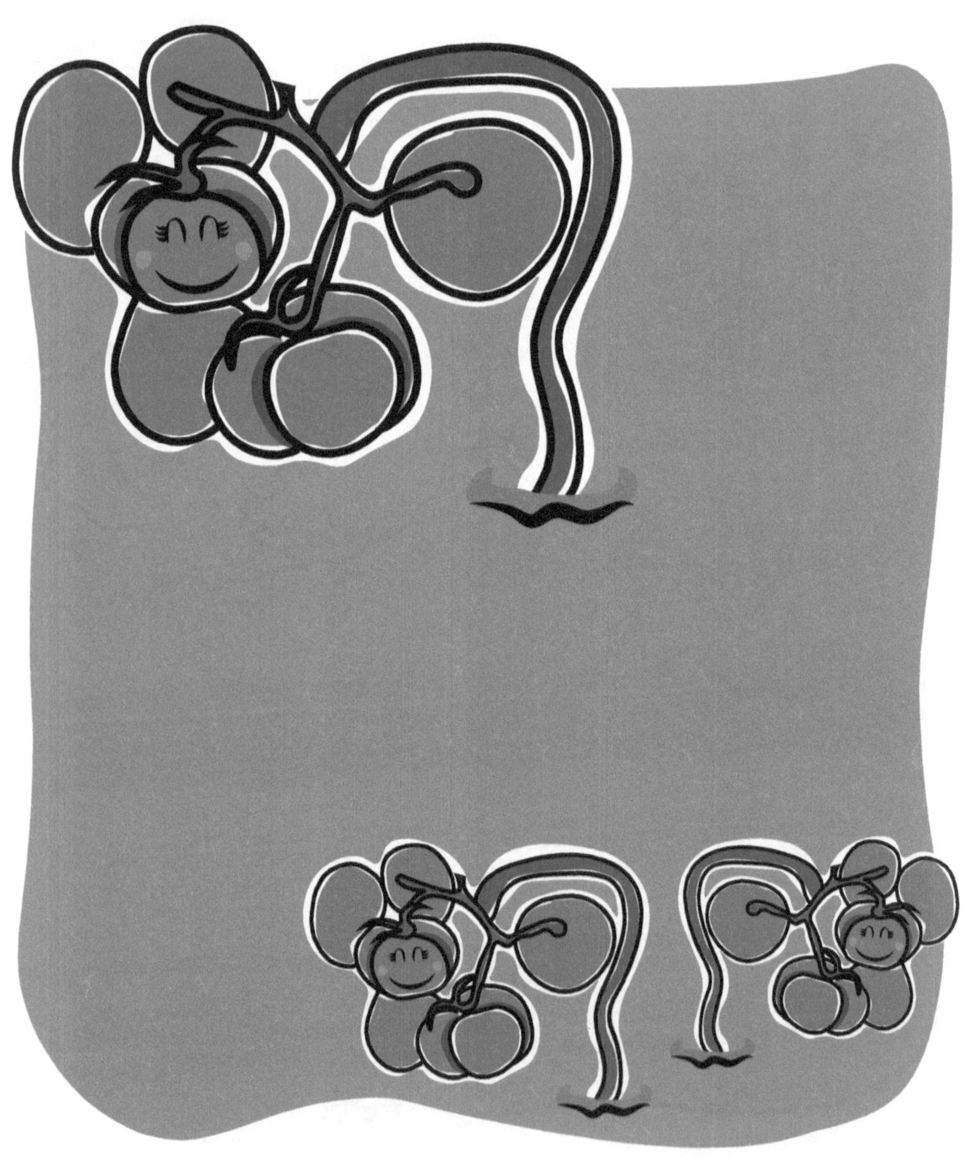

Their brother the Pistachio was taller
than all the others. His various colors,
green, red and brown were so much
like his father`s!

The Eggplant was white and sweet
making all the eggplants of earth feel
jealous of her.

The oldest though and most
successful one was the Vineyard. He
was tough and hardworking, and he
produced the best wine on earth! His
mother was so proud of him!

It seemed that Mr. Volcano was calm and happy after all. Occasionally he was getting angry, and he was throwing out lava, gases, and ash, but these bursts were nothing like that of the Minoan times.

His wife was happy and productive
with him. On his rocky, craggy body
she created exceptional domed nests
for her descendants, and their beauty
soon became legendary and spread out
around the world.

Nowadays they host millions of
visitors who come from all around the
world to admire their great
relationship and unique charm.

Mr. Volcano`s breath is stable and warm, and Humanity feels happy and safe in his arms...

...however, she always has an eye open to notice any sign of her husband`s behavior that would warn her of a potential danger.

Deep inside, she is aware that he is going to wake up again furious some day...